AMERICA IN THE TIME OF
COLUMBUS

From Earliest Times to 1590

Sally Senzell Isaacs

Heinemann Library
Des Plaines, Illinois

Published by Heinemann Library,
an imprint of Reed Educational & Professional Publishing,
1350 East Touhy Avenue, Suite 240 West
Des Plaines, IL 60018.

AMERICA IN THE TIME OF COLUMBUS
was produced for Heinemann Library
by Bender Richardson White.

Editor: Lionel Bender
Designer: Ben White
Assistant Editor Michael March
Picture Researcher: Madeleine Samuel
Media Conversion and Typesetting: MW Graphics
Production Controller: Kim Richardson

03 02 01 00
10 9 8 7 6 5 4 3

Printed in Hong Kong

Library of Congress Cataloging-in-Publication Data.
Isaacs, Sally, 1950–
    America in the time of Columbus : from earliest times to 1590 /
Sally Senzell Isaacs.
        p.   cm.
    Includes bibliographical references and index.
    Summary: Uses the life of Christopher Columbus as a backdrop to
present the history of the people of America from the time the Native
Americans arrived until 1590.
    ISBN 1-57572-742-0 (lib. bdg.). ISBN 1-57572-933-4 (pbk.)
    1. America--History--To 1810--Juvenile literature. 2. Columbus,
Christopher--Juvenile literature.   [1. America--History--To 1810.
2. Columbus, Christopher.]   I. Title.
E187.I83   1998
970.01--dc21   98-21298
                                                                      CIP
                                                                      AC

Special thanks to Mike Carpenter, Scott Westerfield, and Tristan Boyer at
Heinemann Library for editorial and design guidance and direction.

Photo Credits:
Picture Research Consultants, Mass: pages 8 top and 12 bottom (Library
of Congress), 10 top (British Library), 10 bottom (Parks Canada/Shane
Kelly), 12 top and 19 bottom (National Museum of the American Indian), 20
left (The Bancroft Library, Univ. of California, Berkeley), 32 bottom. North
Wind Pictures: page 41 bottom (John Carter Brown Library, Brown Univ.).
Peter Newark's American Pictures: pages 7, 8 bottom, 14, 15, 24, 27
bottom, 34, 35, 36, 38 bottom. Werner Forman Archive: pages 6 (Maxwell
Museum of Anthropology, USA), 16 top (Museum fur Volkerkunde, Berlin),
19 top (Museum of Anthropology, Univ. of British Columbia, Canada), 20
right (Field Museum of Natural History, Chicago), 22 left and 22 right
(Schindler Collection, New York). e.t.archive: pages 16 bottom, 31 bottom
and 37 (New York Public Library), 32 top, 41 top (British Museum). Museo
de Ejército, Madrid, Spain: page 27 top. Michael Holford: pages 28 (Senor
Mujica Gallo, Lima), 31 top (British Museum). Page 38 top: By Courtesy of
the National Portrait Gallery, London.

Every effort has been made to contact copyright holders of any material
reproduced in this book. Omissions will be rectified in subsequent printings
if notice is given to the publisher.

Artwork credits
Illustrations by: John James on pages 6/7, 8/9, 14/15, 20/21, 22/23,
24/25, 26/27, 32/33, 34/35, 40/41; James Field on pages 10/11,
12/13, 18/19, 28/29, 36/37; Mark Bergin on pages 16/17, 38/39;
Gerald Wood on pages 30/31.   All maps by Stefan Chabluk.
Cover: Design and make-up by Pelican Graphics. Artwork by John James.
Photos: Top: Picture Research Consultants, Mass.–Library of Congress.
Center: e.t. archive–New York Public Libary. Bottom: e.t. archive.

Major quotations used in this book come from the
following sources. In some cases, quotes have been
abridged for clarity:
On pages 14, 22: Words from Native American songs are
from Thomas, David Hurst; Miller, Jay; White, Richard;
Nabokov, Peter; and Deloria, Philip J. *The Native
Americans - An Illustrated History.* Atlanta: Turner
Publishing, Inc., 1993. pages 107, 66.
On pages 24, 25, 26: Excerpts from Fuson, Robert H.,
translation of *The Log of Christopher Columbus.* New
York: Tab Books (McGraw Hill), 1971.
On page 32: Quote for Vespucci letter from Faber, Harold
The Discoverers of America. New York: Charles Scribner's
& Sons, 1992. page 92.
On pages 32, 36, 40: Various quotes mentioned in Hakim,
Joy *A History of US – The First Americans.* New York:
Oxford University Press, 1993. pages 85,105,147.

The Consultants
Special thanks go to Diane Smolinski and
Nancy Cope for their help in the preparation of
this series. Diane Smolinski has years of
experience interpreting standards documents
and putting them into practice in fourth and fifth
grade classrooms. Nancy Cope splits her time
between teaching high school history, chairing
her department, training new teachers at North
Carolina State University, and being President-
Elect of the North Carolina Council
for Social Studies.

The Author
Sally Senzell Isaacs is a professional writer and
editor of nonfiction books for children. She
graduated from Indiana University, earning a
B.S. degree in Education with majors in
American History and Sociology. For some
years, she was the Editorial Director of
Reader's Digest Educational Division. Sally
Senzell Isaacs lives in New Jersey with her
husband and two children.

CONTENTS

America in the Time of is a series of nine books arranged chronologically, meaning that events are described in the order in which they happened. However, since each book focuses on an important person in American history, the timespans of the titles overlap. In each book, most articles deal with a particular event or part of American history. Others deal with aspects of everyday life, such as trade, houses, clothing, and farming. These general articles cover longer periods of time. The little illustrations at the top left of each article are a symbol of the times. They are identified on page 3.

▼ **About the map**
This map shows the United States today. It shows the boundaries and names of all the states. Refer to this map, or to the one on pages 42–43, to locate places talked about in this book.

About this book

This book is about America from the time when the earliest people arrived until 1590. The term America means mostly "the United States of America." Some historians refer to the native people of America as Amerinds or as Indians, as Christopher Columbus did. Others call them Native Americans, as we do. Columbus called them Indians because he thought he had reached the East Indies islands of Asia. The islands Columbus landed at were later called the West Indies to distinguish them from the East Indies. Words in **bold** are described in more detail in the glossary on page 46.

INTRODUCTION

At one time, there were no people living on the land we now call America. Then, perhaps 30,000 years ago, the first Americans stepped onto the continent. They were the people we now call Native Americans. They walked over a land bridge from Asia into the northwestern part of North America. Over thousands of years, the people spread out to the south, east, and west.

By the time Christopher Columbus arrived in America in 1492, Native Americans lived throughout North and South America. Columbus himself met various **tribes** of Native Americans who lived 400 miles south of Florida, on islands in the Caribbean Sea.

Columbus returned to Europe with the news of his discovery. Other European explorers set sail for the **New World**. Neither the Americas nor the lives of the Native Americans would ever be the same. By 1600, such European countries as England, Spain, and France were sending people to America to build **colonies**. The Native Americans sometimes helped the newcomers. At other times they fought against them. Most tribes of Native Americans tried to stay on their treasured lands for as long as possible.

Some events in this book took place before Christopher Columbus was born. Other events happened after he died. On pages that describe events during Columbus's life, there are yellow boxes that tell you what Columbus or his family was doing at that time.

THE FIRST AMERICANS

Many thousands of years ago, small animals scurried along river banks. Birds soared through the sky. Huge woolly animals roamed freely. Hunters searching for food followed these animals onto undiscovered land. These hunters were the first Americans.

The first Americans probably arrived between 15,000 and 30,000 years ago. These people did not settle in villages. They kept moving to find new sources of food and shelter. They hunted such large animals as caribou, saber-toothed tigers, and mastodons. When these animals roamed, the hunters followed. This movement from one place to another is called **migration**.

▶ This spearhead was found by **archeologists** in Folsom, New Mexico. It may be 10,000 years old. Archeologists are people who dig up and study objects to learn about the past. They have learned that early hunters in America used sharp stone spearheads.

▶ The first Americans could have walked onto the continent during two different ice ages. One happened 30,000 to 34,000 years ago. Another happened 15,000 to 30,000 years ago.

During these ice ages, the Bering Strait between Alaska and Siberia in Russia became a land bridge. The oceans froze and the land under the sea rose to create a natural bridge between Asia and North America. When the ice ages ended, the ice melted and the sea covered the land bridge.

As the hunters crossed the treeless plains, they set up tentlike houses made of large animal bones covered with furs. They made fires in the center of each house to keep warm.

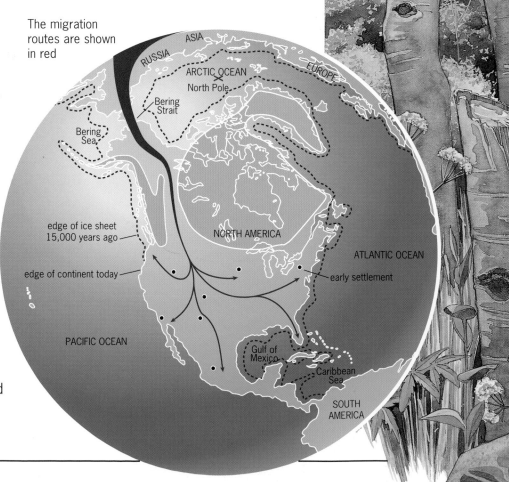

The migration routes are shown in red

ASIA
RUSSIA
ARCTIC OCEAN
North Pole
Bering Strait
Bering Sea
EUROPE
edge of ice sheet 15,000 years ago
NORTH AMERICA
ATLANTIC OCEAN
edge of continent today
early settlement
PACIFIC OCEAN
Gulf of Mexico
Caribbean Sea
SOUTH AMERICA

▲ Inuit Eskimos, like this man in a sketch made in 1822, lived in what today is called Canada and Alaska. The Inuit probably came from Asia by boat after the land bridge melted for the last time.

The hunt

Hunters needed animal meat for food, skins for clothing, and bones to make spears and houses. They traveled in bands of six to eight men. Sometimes hunters chased the animals into swamps. Once trapped, the animals were easier to spear. Women were in charge of cooking the meat and scraping the animal skins to make them into leather.

Over thousands of years, the largest animals died out. Forests grew, replacing the open grasslands where the large animals lived. Many groups of people settled by the forests and hunted smaller animals. They fished in rivers and streams. Some people became farmers. They selected and bred various wild plants and created corn, potatoes, and squash that could be grown in fields.

7

THE MOUND BUILDERS

As archeologists try to reconstruct, or put together, a picture of the earliest Americans, they are finding pieces of the puzzle in earth mounds. Mounds are huge piles of earth made by people. Thousands of mounds have been found across America.

▶ This is an aerial view of Serpent Mound today. It was hidden under a forest in Ohio. It was discovered around 1850 when a tornado ripped out the trees. The snake-shaped mound is 400 yards (366 m) long. It was built about 2,000 years ago by a Native American group called the Adena.

Sites of mound builders

Many groups of mound builders lived in central and eastern America. They built mounds in different shapes. Some were square, others were round. They made some mounds in the shapes of animals such as snakes, turtles, and bears.

Many mounds were used as burial places. People buried gifts and possessions with their leaders. **Archeologists** have found **artifacts** such as pottery, tools, and beaded jewelry in some mounds. These tell us about the everyday lives, skills, crafts, and traditions of the people.

▲ When archeologists find seashells far from the coast, they learn that the people traveled to distant places and traded with other groups. This shell neck-ornament was found in Spiro Mound in present-day Oklahoma. Other artifacts that have been found in Native American burial mounds include stone axes, bone needles, farm tools, wooden masks, and copper bracelets.

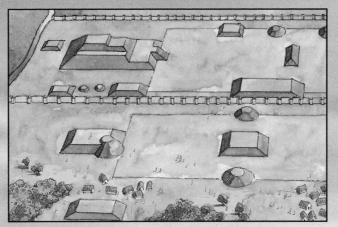

► About 800 years ago, the city of Cahokia stood in present-day Illinois. Nearly 40,000 people lived there. There were streets, markets, and mounds like those shown here. The people built temples on the mounds.

▼ The people of Cahokia lived in huts near the mounds. The leaders had the biggest huts. Workers and farmers had smaller huts. Some people raised livestock and grew corn, beans, and squash. **Slaves** did most of the work.

Lessons in the earth

The size of the mounds shows that the Cahokians must have had good leaders to organize these constructions.
A log and clay fence surrounding the city shows that they protected their city well.

Artifacts also show they enjoyed outdoor games. In one game, players tossed a rock and threw spears to pinpoint where it stopped. The western part of the city, near the Mississippi River, was probably a marketplace. Stone blades, salt, and furs from 400 miles (640 km) away suggest this.

THE VIKINGS

Christopher Columbus was not the first European to reach America. More than 500 years before Columbus arrived, daring explorers came from Sweden, Norway, and Denmark. They were called Vikings, a word which meant "pirates."

Only some Vikings were pirates, but those people could be cruel. In England and France, Viking warriors quietly rowed their ships into shallow rivers. They attacked villages, stealing horses, food, and valuable objects. However, most Vikings were peaceful farmers. They sailed from **Scandinavia** to find better land to raise their crops and animals.

▶ Viking ships were small and swift. Sailors kept their course by following the stars. Above: Since there were no stoves on ship to cook food, salted fish (stored in barrels) was a typical meal. Salting kept food from spoiling. Right: Sailors double up in sleeping bags.

▶ Viking sailors told sagas, or long stories, about stormy Atlantic seas and their fear of being eaten by sea serpents churned up by the waves. The sagas were passed down through the years. They prompted 16th-century artists to draw pictures like this of sea monsters.

▼ In 1964, at L'Anse aux Meadows in Newfoundland, Canada, **archeologists** found remains of eight Viking houses and a tool for spinning wool, dating to A.D. 1000. This photo shows a rebuilt Viking house and boat. Similar houses exist in Labrador in Canada.

A Viking colony

Old stories tell about a Viking colony called Vinland. Some historians think it was in Massachusetts in the United States. Others say it was in Newfoundland, Canada. The stories tell of Leif Erikson, who sailed there in A.D. 1000 and liked the warmer climate and plentiful grape or berry vines. For several years, other Scandinavians followed him to Vinland. Then they all left. No one knows why.

GREENLAND
ICELAND
NORWAY

England

France

Spain

L'Anse aux Meadows
Newfoundland

Nova Scotia

NORTH AMERICA

Atlantic Ocean

◀ Most Vikings were interested in bigger and better farmland. Around A.D. 870, some Vikings left Norway and sailed partway across the Atlantic. They set up villages in Iceland and Greenland. When all the good farmland was used there, they sailed west. By accident, a sailor named Bjarni Herjulfsson became the first known European to see the mainland of North America.

◀ In a Viking village:
• farmers grew crops and raised cows and sheep
• many homes had one room with no windows
• fires were used for cooking, heat, and light
• in homes, people sat and slept on benches.

PEOPLE OF THE NORTHEAST

Deep in the woodlands of the Northeast, Native Americans lived in villages surrounded by tall fences. These people survived by using things provided by nature. They turned trees into homes and earth into farmland.

The woodland groups were **tribes** like the Algonquin, Shawnee, Powhatan, and Iroquois. They all relied on the **natural resources** of the forests. Without forest animals, they would have no food or clothing. Without forest trees, they would have no lumber for homes or boats.

In some areas, people lived in small one-family homes called **wigwams**. In other places, they lived in **longhouses**. Several families, all related to each other, lived in one longhouse. People traveled the rivers in canoes. They made canoes from tree bark laced together with roots.

▼ Hunters in both the Northeast and Southeast wore deer skins to fool the animals. The artist Jacques Le Moyne sketched this picture and Theodore de Bry engraved it in 1591.

▶ When illness struck a family, they would call for a member of the False Face Society. These people wore masks (false faces) and had healing powers. A cured patient had to join the society.

Area of Northeast tribes

▶ When fighting broke out among the Northeastern tribes, warriors used clubs made of wood and stone. They also used bows and arrows.

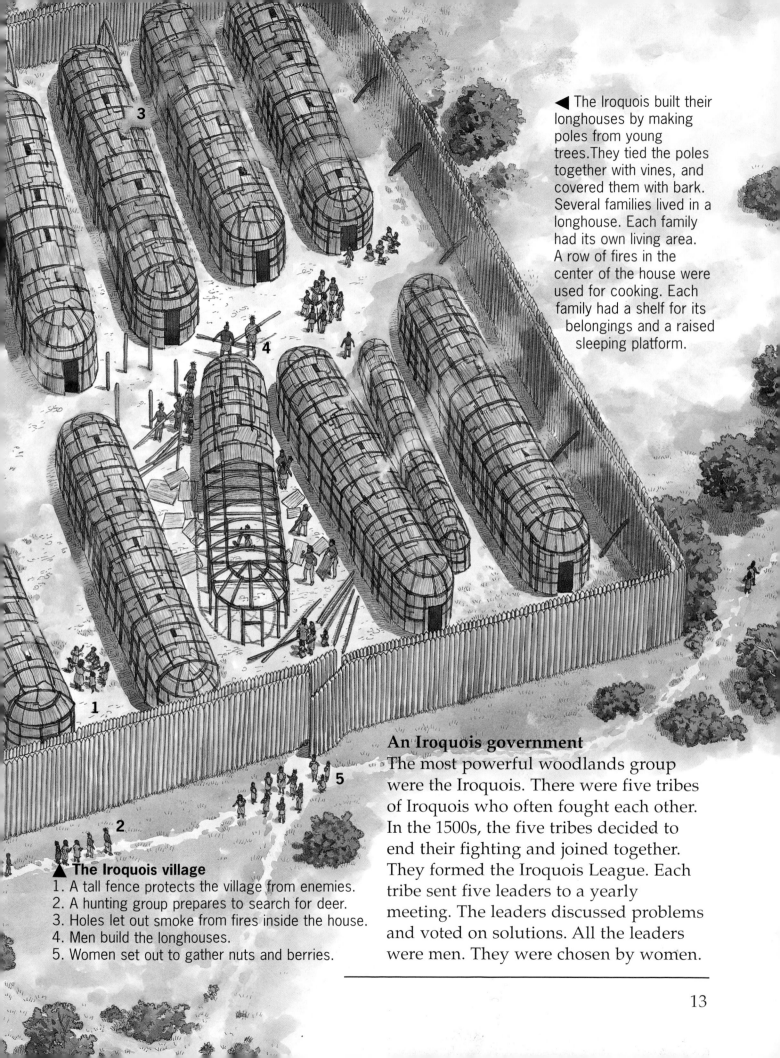

▶ The Iroquois built their longhouses by making poles from young trees. They tied the poles together with vines, and covered them with bark. Several families lived in a longhouse. Each family had its own living area. A row of fires in the center of the house were used for cooking. Each family had a shelf for its belongings and a raised sleeping platform.

An Iroquois government

The most powerful woodlands group were the Iroquois. There were five tribes of Iroquois who often fought each other. In the 1500s, the five tribes decided to end their fighting and joined together. They formed the Iroquois League. Each tribe sent five leaders to a yearly meeting. The leaders discussed problems and voted on solutions. All the leaders were men. They were chosen by women.

▲ **The Iroquois village**
1. A tall fence protects the village from enemies.
2. A hunting group prepares to search for deer.
3. Holes let out smoke from fires inside the house.
4. Men build the longhouses.
5. Women set out to gather nuts and berries.

13

TRIBES OF THE SOUTHEAST

"Behold the wonderful work of our hands: and let us be glad." For generations, the Choctaws have sung these words at their Green Corn Ceremony. Like all tribes of the Southeast, these people were thankful for the rich soil and mild climate of their homeland.

The Southeast people included such **tribes** as the Cherokee, Seminole, and Natchez. Thanks to the warm climate, these people were successful farmers. Men cleared the land. Women planted corn, beans, squash, and pumpkins.

At harvest time, everyone in the village gathered the crops. They celebrated the harvest with the Green Corn Ceremony. For several days, they ate a big feast and danced around a sacred fire. Afterward, one woman from each household took some of the fire back to her home.

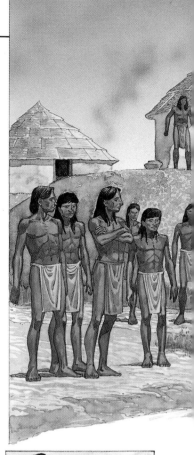

▶ Among the Natchez, the chief of the tribe was called the Great Sun. Priests and war leaders were known as Nobles. Farmers, workers, and captives used as **slaves** were called Stinkards. Here, the Great Sun is carried among the Stinkards. Behind them is a temple and homes, all built on mounds.

▶ A Natchez mother wears a basket on her back for collecting corn.

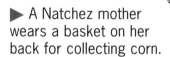

◀ Villages often settled arguments by playing this game. More than 100 players joined each team. Players used two sticks with webbed ends to catch a ball and throw it between the opponent's goalposts. This painting was made by George Catlin around 1835.

▲ This drawing, made by artist Jacques Le Moyne in 1564, shows people taking their crops to be stored in a big barnlike building called a **granary**.

▼ More Native Americans lived here than in any other region north of Mexico. The area includes mountains, seashores, swamps, and pine forests.

Fashions from animal skins

The Southeast tribes were also skilled hunters. Usually using bows and arrows, they hunted deer, turkeys, bears, and buffalo. With the animal skins, they made deerskin shirts, skirts, dresses, and leggings. Body paint, tattoos, and jewelry often completed the fashions. Hairstyles were also important. Some men shaved their heads with sharp shells, leaving only a small clump of hair on top to which they attached feathers.

▼ The Seminoles made **chickees** with the trunks and leaves of palm trees. Because of the hot, humid climate of Florida, the Seminoles built such homes to keep cool and dry. The open sides let a breeze flow through. The floor was raised to avoid flooding during heavy rains.

Area of Southeastern tribes

15

THE GREAT PLAINS TRIBES

The Great Plains are the rolling lands between the Rocky Mountains and the Mississippi River. Native Americans of the eastern plains were farmers and hunters. The western plains were dry and difficult to farm. The people there relied on buffalo to stay alive.

In the summer, the buffalo left the forests and valleys, and gathered in the tall grasses of the western plains. The Native Americans packed their belongings and left their winter villages. They set up camps and prepared for buffalo drives.

Each group of hunters first piled rocks to build a V-shaped path that pointed toward a cliff. At the bottom of the cliff, they built a large fenced-in **corral**. The hunters hid behind the rock piles above the cliff. When the buffalo passed, the hunters jumped out, shouting and waving. The frightened animals ran over the cliff, into the corral, and were killed.

▶ Plains **tribes** made this baby carrier from buffalo skin. They also
• ate the buffalo meat
• made **tepees** and clothing from the skins
• made tools and eating utensils from the horns
• used **sinew** as thread
• burned buffalo dung (droppings) for fuel.

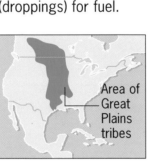

Area of Great Plains tribes

◀ This painting of 1844 by George Catlin shows Great Plains hunters wearing wolf skins so they can sneak up on the buffalo.

The role of women

For many Great Plains tribes, the women took charge of the villages. They made clothing, tepees, and tools. In some groups, women raised the crops and built the winter lodges. In others, they hunted with the men. When the people held their sacred Sun Dance Ceremony, they chose a wise woman to chop down the special tree that was the focus of the ceremony.

Names on the Plains
Some of the Great Plains tribes were the Arapaho, Arikara, Assiniboine, Gros Ventre, Kiowa, Mandan, Osage, Blackfeet, Comanche, Crow, Pawnee, and Sioux. The names of some Great Plains tribes were used for cities and states in the United States: Iowa, Missouri, Kansa(s); Cheyenne, Wichita, Omaha.

▲ Western Great Plains tribes lived in earthen lodges in the winter.

▶ In the summer, the tribes followed the buffalo herds, carrying their homes with them.
• Each family slept in a tepee.
• Dogs dragged a **travois** that held their belongings.
• After the men killed the buffalo, the women scraped the skins and tied them to a wooden frame for drying.
• Buffalo meat was hung over poles to dry.
• Babies spent most of their time on their mothers' backs in a carrier.

WESTERN NATIVE AMERICANS

Area of Northwest tribes
Area of Plateau tribes
Area of Great Basin tribes

Native Americans of the three western areas lived differently. Those of the Plateau mainly gathered roots and bulbs while tribes of the Great Basin found food to be even scarcer. In contrast, the Northwest tribes held feasts to celebrate their plentiful lifestyle.

The people of the Northwest lived along the Pacific Ocean, from Alaska to California. The forests provided plenty of wood to build their homes and fishing boats. The sea provided plenty of food.

Every person belonged to a clan. A clan is a large family including grandparents, aunts, uncles, and cousins. Many clans were named for animals. The people were proud of their clans.

▼ Northwest Native Americans were good artists and builders.
• Many **totem poles** were like family trees. The carvings told of family events, such as marriages, or were built to honor a special person.
• Canoes were pulled onto shore, bringing a catch of fish, sea otters, and seals.
• Houses were made from trees.

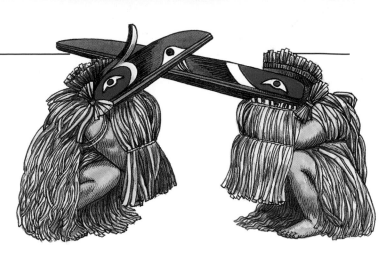

▼ This totem pole was made by the Haida **tribe** of the Northwest region. It shows images of a raven, bear, frog, and wolf.

▶ Clans in the Northwest held a **potlatch** to show off and share their possessions with other clans. People feasted, danced in masks, as shown here, and told family stories.

Native Americans of the Great Basin and Plateau

In the hot desert of the **Great Basin**, food was hard to find. People lived mostly on pine nuts, acorns, rabbits, and sometimes insects. Elsewhere in the region, people also ate fish and birds. They did not build villages. Instead, they wandered, setting up camps during the nut-gathering and rabbit-hunting season.

In the **Plateau**, people spent the summer collecting fish, roots, and berries. They lived in **tepees** that could be set up and taken down quickly. In the winter, they lived in warm houses built partly underground. The roof was rounded, with a hole in the center to let out smoke from the cooking fire. People often entered and left the house through this roof hole. Each family had its own tepee and house.

◀ These two duck decoys were made about 2,000 years ago by Native Americans living in the Great Basin. They were found near the Humbolt River in Nevada.

The decoys are made of dried plant stems and leaves woven together. They were placed on lakes and ponds to attract ducks. The people ate fish, rabbit, and other animals. They made their clothes from animal skins. Rabbit skin robes kept them warm in the winter.

CALIFORNIAN TRIBES

Mild weather, sandy beaches, redwood forests—early Native Americans enjoyed these California resources as much as we do today. They migrated from all over the country to settle in the area. In fact, more languages were spoken here than in any other region.

Compared to Native American groups living east of them, the Californians had an easy life. Cold weather was rare. Most of the time, people wore only small pieces of animal skins. There was no need to farm. More than enough food grew wild or could be hunted. Oak trees grew nearly everywhere, making acorns the main food. People who lived near lakes and rivers speared fish. Those who lived by the ocean caught crayfish, crabs, and mussels. Deer, elk, and rabbits roamed the mountains. Birds flew overhead. The people did not worry about food.

The first Hawaiians arrive
Hawaii is a group of islands in the Pacific Ocean. It has been part of the United States since 1959. About 2,000 years ago, the first people sailed to the islands in giant canoes. They were called Polynesians and they came from other islands in the Pacific Ocean. In about A.D. 1200, Polynesians from the island of Tahiti came to Hawaii and took control from the earlier settlers.

Area of Californian tribes

▶ To collect acorns, Pomo women wore deep baskets on their backs and with long-handled tools they knocked the acorns from the trees into the baskets.

▲ This picture shows a ceremonial dance. These **tribes** painted their bodies and placed feathers in their hair.

▶ This original Pomo basket is decorated with hummingbird, woodpecker, and quail feathers.

Keeping peace

Many small groups of Native Americans lived in California. Usually they got along peacefully. Yet sometimes they fought to protect their land. Some groups posted guards to keep others from fishing in their rivers or taking acorns from their oak trees. To settle an argument, two fighting groups might line up facing each other. Each would send out a single warrior to fight while the others cheered.

◀ A Pomo Village.
• Like many Californian tribes, the Pomo lived in huts. They tied poles together and covered them with tall grass.
• Pomos wove beautiful baskets tight enough to hold water or acorn soup. Baskets were also used as tools, hats, and baby carriers.
• The women ground acorns into meal. Then they pressed the meal into cakes and baked it in open fires.

21

SOUTHWEST DESERT DWELLERS

"The whole Southwest was a House Made of Dawn. It was made of pollen and of rain." These words from a Southwest Native American song draw the picture of the sun-drenched cornfields. Months of dry days were broken by heavy rain.

The Southwest area has steep canyons and jagged cliffs. Native Americans, such as the ancient Anasazi and later the Hopi, Navaho, and Pima, built their homes from the **natural resources** around them. More than 1,000 years ago, the Anasazi built stone villages on top of flat-topped hills called **mesas**. About 900 years ago, people began carving homes into the cliffs. Each community was called a **pueblo**. The people were also called Pueblo.

The Pueblo were clever farmers. When it snowed in the hills, they would roll a snowball from the top of a hill to the village. When the snowball melted, they had water for their crops. They also dug ditches that brought water from the rivers to the fields.

▼ Between A.D.1100 and 1300, the Anasazi built this community into the side of a cliff in Colorado. More than 400 people lived in its 200 rooms. The rooms are small, but the Anasazi spent much of their time outside.

Abandoned pueblos
By the 1400s, many Pueblos in Colorado and Utah had left their cliff villages. Many scientists believe that they moved toward New Mexico because of a 20-year dry spell in Utah and Colorado. Several pueblos can be seen today—the one shown below is in Mesa Verde National Park in Colorado. Pueblo Bonito (opposite), in New Mexico, was named by early Spanish explorers —it is Spanish for "pretty village."

◀ This kachina doll is not a toy. It is the way Southwest Native American children still learn about the spirit world of their people. Kachinas are messengers between the people and the gods. They bring good luck. When boys turn 13 years old, they learn the secrets of the kachina. They can then join the sacred dance.

▶ A unmarried Pueblo girl wound her hair into two tight rolls, one on each side of her head. Married women usually wore their hair in two simple braids.

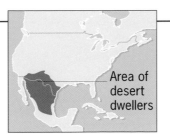

▼ In 950, the Anasazi built Pueblo Bonito, an apartment town in Chaco Canyon, New Mexico. It stood five stories high.

Area of desert dwellers

Corn customs

Corn was the most important crop for the Pueblo. The people had many customs that they felt would bring them a good crop. All newborn babies received an ear of corn which they kept as a charm for the rest of their lives. People also sprinkled cornmeal on their floors for good luck.

◀ Some pueblos had hundreds of rooms. There were rooms in which families slept. There were also meeting rooms, called **kivas**, where men gathered to make laws and hold ceremonies. These homes, built close together into a cliff, were safe from enemy attacks.

23

COLUMBUS ARRIVES!

"I thought I saw a light. It looked like a wax candle bobbing up and down." Columbus wrote this on October 11, 1492, after a 69-day journey across the Atlantic. Land, at last! At daybreak, Columbus grabbed a Spanish flag to claim the land.

Red line on map shows the route of Columbus's first voyage.

The Taíno people called their tiny island Guanahaní. It lay 400 miles (640 km) southeast of present-day Florida, among the islands now called the Bahamas. It is likely that October 12, 1492, was the strangest day in the lives of these people.

At first, someone may have noticed three sets of billowing sails on the horizon. Since they had never seen ocean-going ships, they might have imagined wild sea animals. As the huge monsters came closer, the Taíno recognized them as boats, perhaps "white-sailed canoes."

Soon, odd-looking people rowed to shore in smaller boats. They were dressed in strange clothing. Some had hair growing out of their chins. Then the Taíno learned that Christopher Columbus and three ships of Spanish explorers had arrived.

▲ Most people traveled from Europe to Asia over land. Columbus wanted to sail west to reach Asia. His three ships left Spain on August 3, 1492. They stopped at the Canary Islands for supplies. On October 12 they found land— not Asia, but an island near Florida.

▲ This portrait of Christopher Columbus was painted in 1519, 13 years after his death, by artist Sabastiano del Piombo.

Who was Christopher Columbus? Information about Columbus is not exact. Most people think he was born in 1451, between August 25 and October 31. He was born in Genoa, Italy, and given the name Cristoforo Colombo. Columbus was working on ships by the age of 14. At 25, he moved to Portugal. He and his brother drew and sold maps. In 1479, Christopher Columbus and his wife, Felipa, had a son, Diego. In 1488 his second son, Fernando, was born. In those days, Europeans traveled to the Indies in Asia to get gold, spices, and silk. (The Indies are now called China, Japan, and India.) Travel over land was difficult and dangerous. Columbus wanted to find a water route to the Indies.

► Columbus sailed with three ships, the *Niña*, the *Pinta*, and the *Santa Maria*. They were made of wood and had no engines. The wind filled their enormous sails and pushed them along.

▼ A crew of 90 people sailed on the three ships. They included officers, sailors, a translator, three doctors, a secretary, an accountant, and servants. Columbus kept his course by watching the North Star.

► As soon as Columbus planted the Spanish flag to claim the land, the Taíno hurried down to the beach. In his **log**, Columbus wrote, "They are friendly people." Columbus called the island San Salvador.

Spain's explorer

Before Columbus set out, he needed money for his journey. He first took his plan to King John II of Portugal. The king wanted the riches of Asia, but he thought Columbus's route westward was ridiculous. Columbus took his plan to King Ferdinand and Queen Isabella of Spain. Eventually, the queen gave him the money to sail for Spain's government. In those days, when explorers found new land, they **claimed** it for their country.

THE COLONY AT HISPANIOLA

Columbus left San Salvador, sailed among the nearby islands, and eventually ended up on the island of Hispaniola. He believed he was near the Indies—the land of gold, silk, and jewels. That is why he called the people "Indians." Yet the people were puzzling. They did not wear jewels and silk.

▶ On Hispaniola, Columbus started a **colony**. The Native Americans came to trade with the new settlers. They traded parrots, balls of cotton thread, and tobacco leaves for glass beads and small bells.

Columbus put his men to work searching for gold. When he first arrived at the islands, Columbus wrote: "I have seen a few **natives** who wear a little piece of gold hanging from a hole made in the nose. (I want to) find a king who possesses a lot of gold."

How Columbus found Hispaniola

As Columbus left San Salvador, he was sure that he was just a few miles away from Asia's mainland. On Christmas Eve, the job of steering the *Santa Maria* was given to a boy who had only a little sailing experience. That night, the ship crashed onto a reef near Hispaniola.

▼ Columbus arrived in Spain on March 15, 1493. King Ferdinand and Queen Isabella were delighted with his report, as shown in this 16th-century Spanish painting. They asked Columbus to make another voyage.

The colony and search for gold

Columbus and the crew spent Christmas Day gathering pieces of wood from the wrecked ship. They took the wood ashore and built a tower and fort for a new colony. They called it Villa de la Navidad in honor of Christmas Day.

Columbus left 40 crew members on the island. The crew was happy to stay since they hoped to discover gold mines. The local Native American chief was happy to have the newcomers. He felt they could help him win wars against enemy **tribes**.

Columbus explored the western coast of Hispaniola. There he found enough nuggets of gold to impress people back in Spain. On January 16, 1493, the *Niña* and the *Pinta* began their journey back to Spain to report to the king and queen.

▼ Columbus himself supposedly made these drawings. They show his ships leaving Spain (left), arriving at Hispaniola (center), then sailing among the other islands of the Bahamas (right). The drawings were first printed in Europe in 1494.

Columbus's First Voyage to America 1492
Aug. 3: leaves Spain
Oct. 12: Lands at San Salvador. Meets the Taíno
Oct. 16: discovers an island and names it Fernandina for his king
Oct. 19: discovers an island and names it Isabella for Spain's queen
Oct. 28: lands at Cuba
Dec. 24: wrecks the *Santa Maria*
Dec. 25: lands at Hispaniola
1493
Jan. 16: leaves Hispaniola for Spain
Mar. 15: reaches Spain
Apr. 17: received as a hero in Barcelona, Spain
Sept. 25: begins second voyage

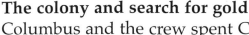

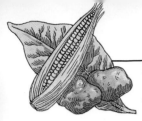

MORE VOYAGES FOR COLUMBUS

Columbus was a hero in Spain. Everyone believed he had discovered islands just off the coast of China and Japan. After much celebration, Columbus was eager to check on his colony at Hispaniola and then begin to find the riches of Asia.

Many people from Spain wanted to travel with Columbus. On September 25, 1493, he went back with 17 ships and 1,200 men. A surprise awaited them at Hispaniola. No one was there! The settlers had mistreated the Native Americans and they had fought back. The settlers also had killed each other in fights over gold and native women. Before long, they had all been killed.

When the new settlers arrived, they found the Native Americans getting sick. Many of them died of diseases that were carried by the Europeans, such as measles. Despite this, Columbus forced the Native Americans to search for gold. He also sent some of them to Spain to be **slaves**.

▶ This gold knife, decorated with turquoise, was made in Peru in about 1250. It is typical of the Native American treasures that proved to Columbus and his men that gold existed in their newly discovered lands. The knife was made by the Chimu people of the Lambayeque region of northern Peru. It was used in religious ceremonies.

▼ In Columbus's day, mapmakers did not know the locations of the continents or the size of the oceans. They only got their information when explorers found the continents and reported back.
  The map on the left shows how Columbus imagined the world. He thought Asia was just across the Atlantic Ocean from Europe. He had no idea that North and South America existed. The map below shows an accurate map of the world marked with the four routes of Columbus's voyages.

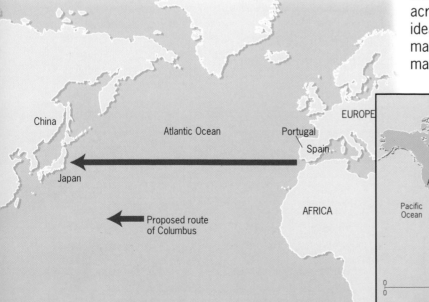

China
Atlantic Ocean
Portugal
Spain
EUROPE
Japan
Proposed route of Columbus

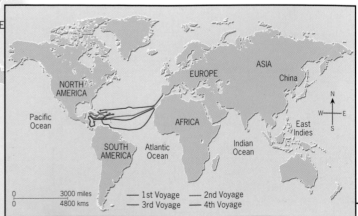

NORTH AMERICA
Pacific Ocean
EUROPE
ASIA
China
AFRICA
SOUTH AMERICA
Atlantic Ocean
Indian Ocean
East Indies
N
W   E
S

| 0 | 3000 miles | — 1st Voyage | — 2nd Voyage |
| 0 | 4800 kms | — 3rd Voyage | — 4th Voyage |

To the New World

The Native Americans learned about new crops that let them feed more people and about guns for hunting and fighting. Europeans introduced the Native Americans to:

- horses, cows, goats, sheep, chickens, pigs
- sugarcane, honey bees
- wheat, barley, oats, rye
- onions, peaches, pears, oranges, olives, bananas
- copper, iron knives.

▼ Columbus's voyages brought together two worlds. The lives of the Native Americans changed forever. Many of them died of diseases. Others lost their land or were forced to be slaves. Yet, new ideas, foods, and goods crossed the ocean. This exchange is called the Columbian Exchange.

To the Old World

Many Europeans got rich by bringing back crops, furs, and metals from the New World. The Native Americans introduced Europeans to:

- corn, potatoes, beans, squash
- chocolate, vanilla, peanuts, cashews
- pineapples, pumpkins, blueberries
- sunflowers, petunias, marigolds
- tomatoes, tobacco, turkeys
- cotton, rubber.

Columbus's Four Voyages

Look at the map on page 28.

Aug. 1492 – Mar. 1493: Sails from Spain to San Salvador, Cuba, and Hispaniola. Starts a **colony** in Hispaniola.

Sept. 1493 – Jun. 1496: Sails back to Hispaniola, but finds no sign of the colony. Forces Native Americans to become slaves.

May 1498 – Oct. 1500: Sails by the coast of South America. New Hispaniola settlers are very unhappy with Columbus's treatment of them. Spain's king and queen send over an officer. He makes Columbus leave Hispaniola.

May 1502 – Nov. 1504: Explores Central America, still finding no sign of Asia. Tired and sick, he ends his search.

More trouble

On his second voyage, Columbus explored more islands. Meanwhile, many of his new settlers were returning to Spain and complaining: "There were no riches. The Native Americans were being treated badly. Columbus was a bad commander."

Columbus sailed back to Spain to defend himself. When he was ready for his third trip, few people wanted to come along. On the third trip, he explored the coast of South America. Still, he found no gold.

The last voyage

On Columbus's last journey, a hurricane damaged his four ships at sea. He sailed along the coast of Central America.

He heard about a large body of water just a few day's walk across the **Isthmus of Panama.** If he had gone, he would have been the first European to see the Pacific Ocean. Instead, Columbus sailed into every bay. He could not find Asia. He felt like a failure. However, without realizing it, he had discovered the "**New World**."

MORE EXPLORERS

For hundreds of years, people in Europe lived and died without ever leaving their villages. Columbus's voyages changed this. There was new land to be discovered. It was no longer a "small world." Many countries began sending explorers across the sea.

England, Spain, Portugal, and France hurried to send out explorers. Explorers had to be good sailors. They also had to be brave. They sailed for weeks to unknown places. In the middle of the ocean, there was no turning back. They had to face the dangers of winds, storms, and darkness.

John Cabot explores Canada

John Cabot sailed from England in 1497 and 1498. He explored the Northeast Coast of North America, now part of Canada. Like Columbus, Cabot thought he was exploring Asia. He, too, found no gold or jewels. On his second voyage, something went terribly wrong. Cabot and his four ships disappeared.

▼ Among the crew, only the captain had a cabin of his own. Each morning, someone woke him and brought him a bucket of water for washing.

Columbus dies

On May 20, 1506, Columbus died in Spain. He was 55 years old. After his fourth voyage, he had become quite sick.

Queen Isabella had died in 1504. Columbus had to argue with King Ferdinand to get most of the money owed him for his travels.

Columbus died a frustrated man. He did not find the Indies or any gold. However, he did sail into unknown territory and many others followed him.

▶ A sailor's day began with scrubbing the ship's **decks**. Next came morning prayers. His many jobs included taking turns to make sure the ship was on course, opening and rolling up sails, and repairing ropes. A noon meal was the only hot meal of the day. The day ended with more prayers. Sailors slept wherever they could.

Parts of a ship:
1. stern (rear) lamp
2. captain's cabin
3. rudder
4. rigging
5. main mast
6. cannon
7. hold
8. anchor
9. fore castle

▶ The ship carried spare sails and supplies in the hold. Animals were sometimes carried on deck to be eaten as fresh meat. Water and wine were stored in barrels or storage jars.

Vasco da Gama crosses the sea to Asia

In 1497, Vasco da Gama left Portugal, at first sailing west. He sailed around the southern tip of Africa and then east to India. He had found a water route to Asia.

The explorations of Juan Ponce de León

In 1513, Juan Ponce de León explored Puerto Rico and **claimed** it for Spain. He then became one of the first explorers to claim part of the mainland of North America. He named the land Florida, which means "full of flowers" in Spanish.

▲ Sailors used this astrolabe to measure the sun's angle above the horizon and to figure out how far north or south of the equator they were.

▶ Europeans forced Native Americans to become their **slaves**. This picture, made in the 1500s, shows slaves carrying Spanish explorers' equipment. By 1502, Europeans used slaves to grow crops in the Bahamas. Then they began to buy slaves in Africa and ship them to the **colonies** in America.

5

6

9

8

7

◀ This is an example of a Spanish or Portuguese explorer's ship in the early 1500s. It was only 100 feet (30 m) long.

THEY CALLED IT AMERICA

Christopher Columbus discovered a new land. Why was this not then called Columbusland or Columbia? It was another explorer who first decided that the land Columbus found was not part of Asia. It was a whole new continent. That explorer was Amerigo Vespucci.

In 1498, Amerigo Vespucci was a merchant in Spain. Columbus bought supplies from Vespucci and shared stories about his trips. Vespucci decided to become an explorer himself. He wrote a letter to his friend, Piero Sodernini. He said, "I decided to...devote myself to more praiseworthy things...and observe a part of the world and its wonders."

▶ Vespucci went to the land we now call South America, and saw the Amazon River (below). He wrote, "I have found a continent more densely peopled and abounding in animals than our Asia or Europe or Africa." He was sure he had found a new continent. Columbus had already been there, but he thought it was part of Asia.

Where Columbus is buried
1506: After his death, Christopher Columbus was buried in the town of Valladolid, Spain.
1509: His son, Diego, moved the body to Seville, Spain.
1526: Diego died and was buried next to his father.
1542: Diego's wife had the remains of Christopher and Diego moved to a special chapel in Hispaniola. Christopher Columbus's last great-grandson died in 1578 with no sons to carry on the family name.

▲ Waldseemüller drew a new world map and added Vespucci's picture and the name "Americi." Later mapmakers realized that there were actually two continents: South America and North America.

▼ As they defend their city of Tenochtitlán, Aztec warriors (right) attack Spanish soldiers.

Drawing a new view of the world

It was mapmaker Martin Waldseemüller who first used the name America. He was interested in Amerigo Vespucci's writings about the new continent or "**New World.**" In 1507, Waldseemüller printed a revised map of the world. He drew in the southern continent that Vespucci described. Then he wrote the word "Americi" in honor of Amerigo Vespucci.

Cortés attacks the Aztecs in Mexico

Meanwhile, the Aztec people were about to have their world turned upside down. They lived in that part of North America we now call Mexico. In 1521, Hernando Cortés from Spain marched his soldiers toward the wealthy Aztec capital city, Tenochtitlán. They burned down the city, killed most of the Aztecs, and sent all the gold and silver back to Spain. Cortés built a new city and called it Mexico City. He called the land around it New Spain.

◄ In 1519, Ferdinand Magellan sailed west from Spain. He sailed around South America into the Pacific Ocean. After three months, he reached the Asian islands of the Philippines. He died there, but his crew sailed on to Spain. They had sailed around the world!

THE FRENCH IN AMERICA

By 1524, the king of France was determined to reach the riches of Asia. By now, he knew that America sat between Europe and Asia. He also knew from Magellan's voyage that sailing around South America to Asia took too long. He had another idea. He wanted someone to find a waterway that cut through America.

▶ In 1562, Jean Ribaut led a group of French people to America, hoping for religious freedom. They started a **colony** called Charlesfort in present-day South Carolina. They built log cabins and grew crops in fields they made near the fort.

▲ The French had heard rumors that Florida was "rich in gold." They hurried to Florida and put the Native Americans to work. This picture of 1563 by Jacques le Moyne de Morgues shows the Native Americans collecting gold from a river using hollow plant stems. This picture may not be accurate.

King Francis I of France sent out Giovanni da Verrazano to look for a waterway through America to the Pacific. He called this the **Northwest Passage**. The country that could **claim** the passage would control the route to Asia and its riches.

In 1524, Verrazano sailed up the coast of North America. He passed what is now North Carolina, Virginia, and Maryland. He sailed into a harbor by today's New York City. He found no passageway so he kept sailing north to Canada.

Ribaut described the land around Charlesfort as "the fairest, fruitfullest, and pleasantest in all the world." But the settlers failed at growing crops and began to starve to death. Desperate to leave, they built ships, using their shirts for sails. At sea, they ran out of food. They were rescued by English ships. Only a few survived and reached France.

Cartier claims New France

King Francis I would not give up. In 1534, he asked Jacques Cartier to search for the Northwest Passage. Cartier sailed up the coast of North America to Canada. There, he discovered the St. Lawrence River. He was sure that the river would take him across North America into the Pacific Ocean.

Cartier explored Canada for several years. At one point, he climbed a mountain and wrote: "One sees a very great distance." He named the peak *Mont-Réal*, French for "royal mountain." This site became the Canadian city of Montreal. Cartier had no luck continuing through the continent. He reached a rapid in the St. Lawrence River where the water raced across the rocky river bottom. His ship could not pass. He turned around.

▼ This North American explorer's map of 1546 shows Jacques Cartier landing in Canada in 1542. Cartier did not find a Northwest Passage. However, he did claim a large area of land for France. He called it New France.

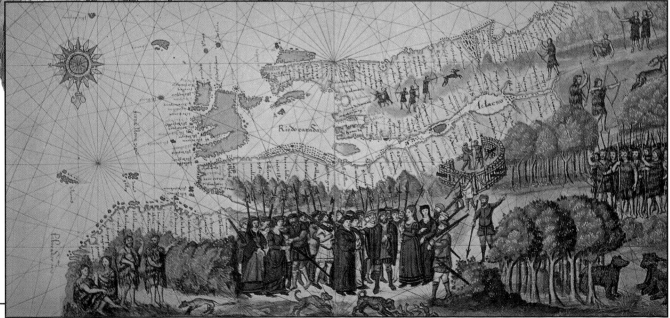

THE SPANISH IN AMERICA

Ever since Columbus sailed to America, Spanish explorers returned again and again. For many of them, America was just a place to get around to reach Asia. By the early 1500s, explorers had other ideas. Maybe there were more riches in America than in Asia.

Spanish Explorers
1513: Ponce de León explores Florida
1521: Hernando Cortés conquers the Aztec empire in Mexico
1528: Narváez explores Florida's southwest coast
1531: Pizarro conquers the Inca empire in Peru
1536–39: Estevanico and Friar Marcos explore Texas and New Mexico
1540–47: Coronado explores the Southwest
1541: De Soto reaches the Mississippi River

▶ Francisco Pizarro could not wait to get to Peru, in South America, and conquer the Inca people. He had heard that the walls of the temples were covered with gold and silver. In 1531, he arrived in Peru with 167 soldiers. The Inca ruler, Atahualpa, and 3,000 followers came to meet Pizarro. The Spaniards fired a cannon and charged forward with swords and guns. Most of the Incas were killed and Atahualpa was taken prisoner.

There was a Spanish legend about The Seven Cities of Gold, also called Cíbola. Spaniards in Mexico began hearing rumors that Cíbola was just north of Mexico. Many left Mexico to explore Florida, Texas, and New Mexico. These Spanish explorers were called **conquistadors**. They were conquerors of new lands.

One conquistador was Estevanico. He was a **slave** from Africa. In 1539, Estevanico and a priest, Friar Marcos, were searching for Cíbola, probably near present-day New Mexico. Friar Marcos asked Estevanico to travel ahead. If Estevanico heard of gold, he should send back messengers with a small cross. According to a report of 1582, Friar Marcos said, "messengers ...returned unto me with a cross as high as a man." Then a messenger came with news that Estavanico had been killed by Pueblo people. Soon after, Friar Marcos returned to Mexico.

▲ The Aztecs made beautiful items out of gold. Cortés melted down many of these to make them easier to carry. As a result, much of the finest Aztec art was lost forever. The gold was taken back to Spain in ships.

▶ Saint Augustine, the oldest town in the United States, looked like this in 1565. In the 1500s, the **settlement** was Spain's military headquarters.

The first permanent colony

Many Spanish explorers passed through Florida in search of gold. In 1565, Spain's king sent Pedro Menéndez de Avilés to start a **colony** in Florida. First Menéndez drove the French out of Fort Caroline. Then he set up Saint Augustine. This was the first permanent European settlement in what is now the United States.

▲ Jean Ribaut of France built this settlement, Fort Caroline, in 1565. It is near present-day Jacksonville, Florida. In 1565, the Spanish king sent Pedro Menéndez de Avilés to take over the fort for Spain. After a horrible, bloody battle, Spain's army won. Menendez wrote a letter to his king: "I had Juan Riboa (Jean Ribaut) and all the rest put to the knife." This engraving was made in 1591.

37

ENGLAND SENDS FRANCIS DRAKE

Queen Elizabeth I of England was envious of Spain. Spain now had colonies in South America. The colonies were rich with gold and silver. England had many daring sailors. The queen allowed them to go and capture Spain's riches—any way they could.

England's daring sailors were called Sea Dogs. Like Spain's **conquistadors**, they wanted to become rich. Francis Drake was perhaps the boldest Sea Dog. He did not bother searching for gold. Instead he let Spain find the gold. Then he stole it!

In 1577, Drake took Magellan's route south around America. He attacked some Spanish towns on the coasts of South and Central America, stealing everything valuable. Then he attacked Spanish ships and took gold, silver, and jewels worth more than $500 million at today's prices.

Explorers after Drake
1576–78: Martin Frobisher explores northern Canada
1583 Humphrey Gilbert claims Newfoundland (Canada) for Elizabeth I
1603–15: Samuel de Champlain brings settlers to Nova Scotia (Canada) and Quebec (Canada)
1609: Henry Hudson explores the Hudson River from the sites of New York City to Albany, New York

▲This portrait of Drake, made by an unknown artist in 1585, shows him with a globe.

▼ Francis Drake's ship *Golden Hind* draws up beside the Spanish treasure ship *Cacafuego*. Drake's sailors boarded the ship, stole the treasures, and sailed away. *Golden Hind* was about 100 feet (30 m) long and carried 18 guns.

▶ Drake made later voyages to America. In 1585, he made several raids on Spanish fortified towns, as here at San Domingo on the island of Hispaniola. Drake's fleet is anchored outside the harbor.

The Spanish called Drake "El Draque," the Dragon, on account of his fierce attacks on their **colonies**.

On the same voyage, Drake may have picked up starving colonists from Roanoke Island (now in North Carolina).

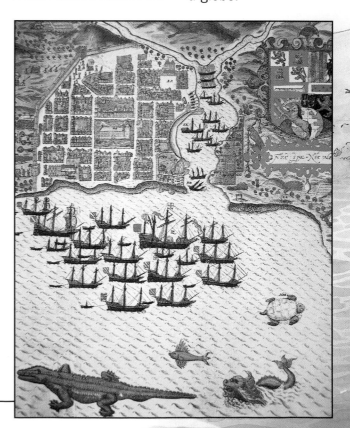

Drake in California

After raiding Spain's ships, Drake was afraid to turn around and sail east back to home. Spanish warships were looking for him. Instead, he kept sailing north in the Pacific Ocean. In 1579, he landed in California, near San Francisco. He named the place Nova Albion. (Albion means "England" in Greek.) Today it is called Drake's Bay.

Drake and his crew received a friendly welcome from the Native Americans. They stayed a month, repairing their ships and taking on supplies. Drake hung a brass plate on a tree to **claim** the land for England.

▶ Near San Francisco, Drake and his crew get into a smaller boat and row to shore. Their ship had been sailing for over 18 months and was badly in need of repairs. They returned to England in 1580.

39

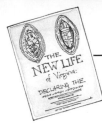

THE LOST COLONY OF ROANOKE

The advertisement read: "The New Life of Virginea." Anyone wishing to move from England to the New World was promised "all the privelges of free... persons native of England." Many people were ready for a new life. Still, the future was unknown.

Sir Walter Raleigh had permission from the queen of England to start a new **colony** in America. In 1585, he brought 7 ships and 100 men to Roanoke Island, in present-day North Carolina.

The **New World** shocked the colonists. They could not grow enough food. When Francis Drake stopped on the island, the settlers sailed back to England with him. In 1587, Raleigh tried again. He brought 91 men, 17 women, and 9 children to Roanoke. Their leader was John White. This colony, too, was doomed.

▶ All that was left of the Roanoke colony were these letters on a tree: CROATOAN—the name of a northern island and Native Americans.

▶ Settlers arrive at Roanoke Island in July 1587 with high hopes. Some left England to get away from crowded cities. Some hoped to become rich. Others wanted more freedom. They brought food and supplies with them, but not enough. In August 1587, their leader, John White, sailed back to England to get more food and supplies. He did not return for three years as all of England's ships were needed to fight the war with Spain.

40

John White was also an artist. This drawing by him from 1590 shows the wife of a Native American chief and her daughter aged about 10. The girl holds a doll dressed as a colonist female.

John White and the Lost Colony

The Roanoke colonists of 1587 built log houses and a fort. John White's daughter, Eleanor, gave birth to the first English child born in what is now the United States. Her name was Virginia Dare.

John White soon sailed to England to get more supplies, and the colonists planned to make their **settlement** grow. But when White returned in 1590, the colonists had vanished. He found only grass, rotted and burned trees, and natives' footprints.

On a tree, White found the word CROATOAN carved into the wood. Perhaps the local Croatan tribe killed everyone? Or, maybe the settlers joined the Native Americans and moved to the nearby island of Croatoan? Because of harsh weather, White could not sail to the island, and returned to England.

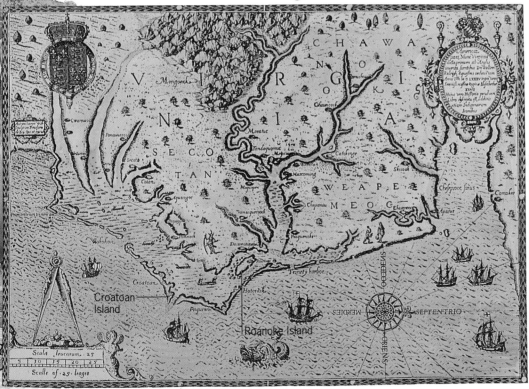

Roanoke Island sits inside an inlet of the Atlantic Ocean. Many ships wrecked on the long, skinny islands in front of Roanoke. In fact, part of White's 1590 search party drowned in these dangerous waters. This map was drawn in 1590 by John White.

Today visitors to Roanoke Island can see Fort Raleigh National Historic Site. The fort was built in 1585 by the first group of settlers. There is also a stone that honors the birth of Virginia Dare, White's granddaughter.

Historical Map of America

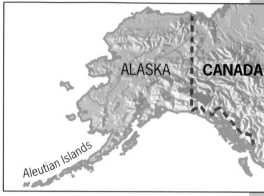

ALASKA | CANADA

Aleutian Islands

PACIFIC OCEAN

On the map
This map shows what was happening in and around North America up to 1590. From about 10,000 years ago, groups of Native Americans lived throughout the land that would become the United States. In A.D. 1000, the Vikings sailed past the northeastern coast. Nearly 500 years later, Christopher Columbus discovered an island off the southeast coast. From then on, many Europeans explored the waters around and within the continent. Some tried to set up colonies, but most failed.

NORTHWEST NATIVE AMERICANS

R O C K Y

Columbia

PLATEAU NATIVE AMERICANS

Drake

Snake

CALIFORNIAN NATIVE AMERICANS

GREAT BASIN NATIVE AMERICANS

M O U N T A I N S

Colorado

Colorado

Rio Grande

Coronado

SOUTHWEST NATIVE AMERICANS

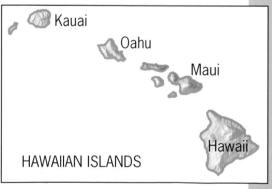

Kauai

Oahu

Maui

Hawaii

HAWAIIAN ISLANDS

Santiago ○

~ River

0	250	500 miles
0	400	800 kilometers

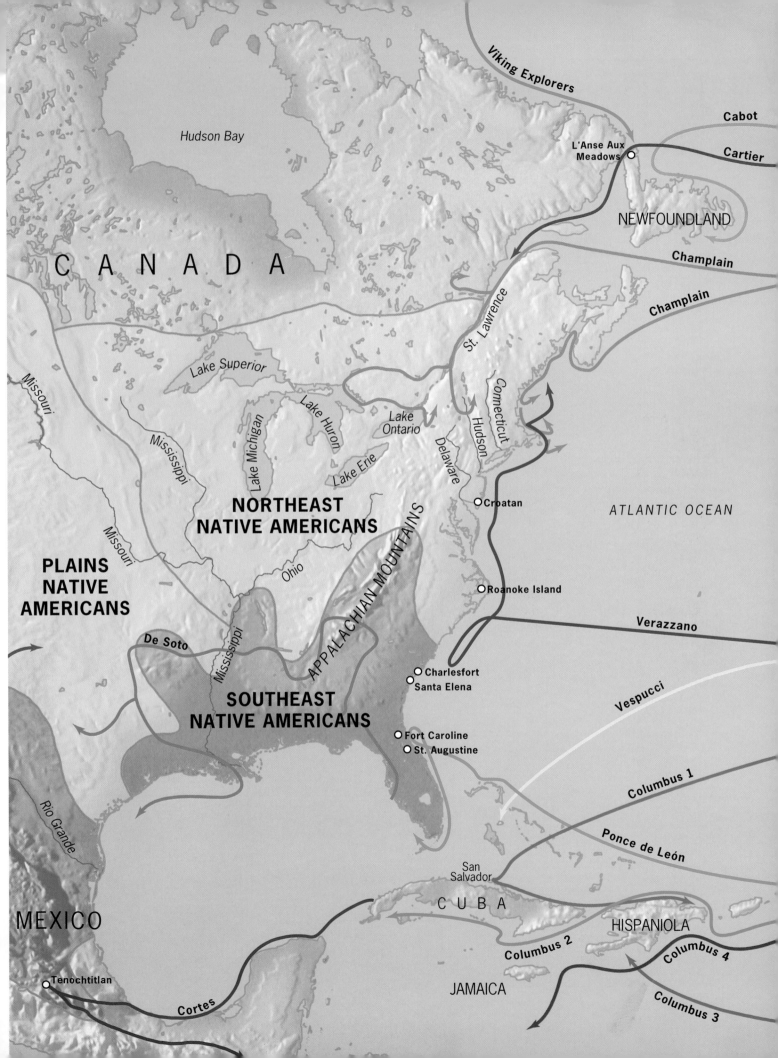

Hudson Bay

Viking Explorers

Cabot

Cartier

L'Anse Aux
Meadows

NEWFOUNDLAND

Champlain

Champlain

C A N A D A

St. Lawrence

Lake Superior

Missouri

Mississippi

Lake Michigan

Lake Huron

Lake Erie

Lake Ontario

Connecticut

Hudson

Delaware

Croatan

ATLANTIC OCEAN

NORTHEAST
NATIVE AMERICANS

Missouri

Ohio

APPALACHIAN MOUNTAINS

Roanoke Island

Verazzano

PLAINS
NATIVE
AMERICANS

De Soto

Mississippi

Charlesfort
Santa Elena

Vespucci

SOUTHEAST
NATIVE AMERICANS

Fort Caroline
St. Augustine

Columbus 1

Ponce de León

Rio Grande

San
Salvador

Columbus 2

MEXICO

C U B A

HISPANIOLA

Tenochtitlan

Columbus 4

JAMAICA

Cortes

Columbus 3

FAMOUS PEOPLE OF THE TIME

Atahualpa, 1500?–33, was the last ruler of the Inca empire in Peru. His empire was conquered and most of his treasures stolen by Pizarro.

Balboa, Vasco Nuñez de 1475?–1519, was a Spanish conquistador who discovered the Pacific Ocean. While in Central America in 1513, friendly Native Americans led him across the Isthmus of Panama. He spotted the ocean and claimed it and its shores for Spain.

Cabeza de Vaca, **Alvar Nuñez** 1490?–1557?, explored Florida for Spain. After a shipwreck in 1528, he wandered through southwestern North America, meeting Pueblo Native Americans. His stories began the legend of The Seven Cities of Gold.

John Cabot, 1450?–1498?, was the first person from England to sail to North America. Sailing for England, he explored the east coast of Canada.

Cabral, **Pedro Alvares** 1467?–1520?, was headed for Asia when he landed in Brazil (South America). He claimed it for Portugal.

Cabrillo, **Juan Rodríguez** ?–1543, led the first European exploration of California. Sailing for Spain in 1542, he reached San Diego Bay and San Francisco Bay.

Jacques Cartier, 1491–1557, discovered the St. Lawrence River in Canada and explored the surrounding land.

Samuel de Champlain, 1567–1635, explored Canada for France and brought settlers to Nova Scotia and Quebec. His group explored the United States as far west as Wisconsin.

Christopher Columbus, 1451–1506, is credited with discovering America and the New World because he was the first European to visit islands off the coast of North America. However, he believed he had reached islands in Asia.

Francisco Coronado, 1510–54, was a Spanish explorer and the first European to explore Arizona and New Mexico.

Hernando Cortés, 1485–1547, was a Spanish conquerer of the Aztec empire in Mexico.

Virginia Dare, 1587?–?, was the first child born of English parents in America. She was born on Roanoke Island and disappeared with the other members of the colony— now called the Lost Colony.

Sir Francis Drake, 1540–1596, was the first English person to sail around the world. He made many voyages to America,

IMPORTANT DATES AND EVENTS

NATIVE AMERICANS
28,000 to 13,000 B.C. First Americans crossed the land bridge from Asia
8000 B.C. land bridge is melted and heaviest migrations into North America end
4000 B.C. Most people in America have stopped hunting big animals. They plant foods, fish, and hunt smaller animals
600 B.C. Adena people begin building mounds in Ohio
A.D. 900 Anasazi people begin building apartmentlike dwellings, called pueblos
A.D. 1200s Cahokia mounds are completed in Illinois
1300s Aztecs move into Mexico
1400s Inca empire expands in Peru
1570 Five Iroquois nations form League of the Iroquois.

EXPLORERS AND SETTLEMENTS
1000 Leif Erikson lands at Newfoundland
1492 Columbus reaches America
1497 Da Gama finds water route to Asia by sailing around the southern tip of Africa
1501 Vespucci explores South America
1513 De León claims Puerto Rico and Florida for Spain
1519 Magellan leads group that is first to sail around the world
1521 Cortés conquers Aztecs in Mexico
1524 Verrazano sails up coast of North America
1531 Pizarro conquers Incas in Peru
1534–1535, 1541–1542 Cartier sails up the St. Lawrence River
1536 Estevanico and Friar Marcos start exploring Texas and New Mexico
1540–1547 Coronado explores Southwest of North America
1541 De Soto reaches the Mississippi River
1562 Ribaut leads French group to start colony of Charlesfort, South Carolina
1565 Pedro Menéndez de Avilés begins colony at Saint Augustine, Florida
1576–1578 Frobisher explores northern Canada for England
1579 Drake lands in California
1587 Raleigh begins second try at Roanoke colony, in North Carolina
1590 White returns to Roanoke colony and discovers that everyone has disappeared.

helping to set up colonies and fighting with the Spanish for treasure.

Leif Erikson, A.D.980?–1025?, was a Viking explorer who may have discovered America when he reached the island of Newfoundland in Canada.

Estevanico, 1500?–1539, was a Black slave who explored the Southwestern United States.

Martin Frobisher, 1535?–1594, was an English explorer who explored northern Canada, thinking it was Asia.

Gama, Vasco da 1469–1524, was a Portuguese explorer and the first European to travel to Asia by sea.

Sir Humphrey Gilbert, 1537?–1583, was Walter Raleigh's half-brother.

In 1576, he argued that there was a Northwest Passage—a waterway through North America linking the Atlantic and Pacific Oceans.(Today, we know there is a Northwest Passage.) In 1583, he claimed Newfoundland (Canada) for England.

Henry Hudson, ?–1611, explored for England and Holland from 1607–1611. He claimed the Hudson River and nearby land for Holland (the Netherlands).

Ferdinand Magellan, 1480–1521, was leader of the first group of explorers to sail around the world.

Menéndez de Avilés, Pedro 1519–1574, set up the first permanent European colony in the United States.

Montezuma, 1466?–1520, was the Aztec ruler

in Mexico. Cortés, from Spain, captured him, stole his treasures, and then took over his empire.

Francisco Pizarro, 1476–1541, was the Spanish conquerer of the Inca people of Peru. He was one of the first conquistadors.

Ponce de León, Juan 1474–1521, was a Spanish explorer who discovered Florida.

Sir Walter Raleigh, 1554?- 1618, was an English navigator and explorer who tried to start a colony at Roanoke Island, North Carolina.

Jean Ribaut, 1520?–1565, tried to build French colonies in South Carolina and Florida.

Soto, Hernando De 1500?–1554, was a Spanish explorer. He

worked in Peru with Pizarro, then he led a group to Georgia, the Carolinas, Tennessee, Alabama, and Oklahoma. He was the first European to see the Mississippi River.

Verrazano, Giovanni da 1480–1527, explored the coast of North America for France.

Amerigo Vespucci, 1454–1512, explored South America and realized it was a different continent from Asia. The name "America" was given to the whole continent—North and South combined—to honor him.

John White, ?–? (late 1500s), was the leader of the colony at Roanoke Island, now known as the Lost Colony.

? means that historians are not sure of the exact date.

COLUMBUS
1451 born in Genoa, Italy
1476 moves to Portugal
1479 marries Doña Felipa Perestrello y Moniz
1484 King of Portugal says "No" to sponsoring Columbus's voyage
1486 Requests that king and queen of Spain sponsor the voyage. They say "Yes" in 1492
1492 discovers Bahamas in America
1493 second voyage to America
1498 third voyage to America
1502 last voyage to America
1506 dies in Vallodolid, Spain

WORLD EVENTS
28,000 to 13,000 B.C. Great Ice Age
8000 B.C. ice melts
3000 to 700 B.C. Ancient Egyptian and Ancient Chinese empires
2500 B.C. first city states in Mesopotomia, western Asia
2000 B.C. agriculture develops in Southeast Asia
1800 to 600 B.C. Assyrian and Babylonian empires in the Middle East
1500 to 400 B.C. Olmec empire in Central America
1200 to 500 B.C. Chavin and Nazca empires in South America
800 to 150 B.C. Ancient Greek empire
600 to 200 B.C. Persian empire
500 B.C. to A.D. 1000 Maya and Toltec empires in Central America
150 B.C. to A.D. 400 Roman Empire becomes the largest in the world

A.D.
100 to 400 Axum empire in Northern Africa
450 to 1000 Saxons, Angles, Jutes, Huns, Visogoths, Celts, then Normans, and Moors dominate Europe and western Asia
1000 to 1450 The Middle Ages or Medieval Period in Europe
1200 to 1520 Inca empire in South America
1200 to 1500 Mongol and Ming empires in China
1300 to 1520 Aztec empire in Central America
1450 Renaissance Period starts. England, France, Italy, Portugal, Holland, and Spain start overseas exploration and setting up colonies.

GLOSSARY

archeologist scientist who digs up objects to study the past

artifact object made or left by people who lived long ago

chickee home built by Native Americans in warm climates. The floor is raised and the sides are open to allow breezes to pass through.

claim announce that something belongs to you or your country

colony place where settlers live far from the country that governs them

conquistador Spanish conqueror who wanted to control new land

corral enclosure, or pen, to keep animals in

deck floor of a ship

granary building used for storing grain

Great Basin part of North America that includes Nevada, Utah, Oregon, Wyoming, Idaho, and Colorado

irrigation bringing water to farmland from rivers and other sources. Pipes and channels may be used to carry the water.

Isthmus of Panama narrow strip of land that joins North and South America

kiva special room used for ceremonies and meetings by the Pueblo Native Americans

lodge permanent home, such as a cabin or house

log notes about a journey written by the captain or leader

longhouse large house in which several Native American families lived

mesa hill or mountain with steep sides and flat top

migration movement from one place to another, usually to find food or shelter

mound pile of earth or hill

native person born in the country

natural resources things that are provided by nature and useful to people, for example timber, metals, water, and soil

New World name given by Europeans in the 1500s to the continents of North and South America. Contrasts with the Old World—the continents of Europe, Africa, and Asia that were known to Europeans at the time.

Northwest Passage water route through North America, above the Arctic Circle, from the Atlantic to the Pacific Oceans.

plains wide area of flat or gently rolling land. The Great Plains is a vast region of the western United States.

plateau large, flat area of land that is higher than surrounding land

potlatch ceremonial feast of Northwest Native Americans in which property was displayed, given away, or destroyed

pueblo Spanish word for village. Also the name of a Native American group.

Scandinavia a region of northern Europe made up of Norway, Denmark, and Sweden. Iceland and Finland are sometimes included.

The Vikings came from Scandinavia.

settlement newly built small village in an area with few people

sinew part of the body that connects muscles; is used as a tether.

slave person who is owned by another person and is usually made to work for that person

tepee tentlike shelter made of animal skins. It could be set up and taken down quickly. (Also spelled tipi or teepee.)

totem pole wooden pole that is carved or painted and shows animals, plants, and objects that represent a family.

travois type of sled used to carry belongings, often pulled by an animal

tribe group of people who share a territory, language, customs, and laws

wigwam small single-family house built of branches and covered with bark or hide. Made by Native Americans.

HISTORICAL FICTION TO READ

Dorris, Michael. *Morning Girl.* New York: Hyperion, 1992.—The story of a Taíno girl and her brother, set in 1492, just before the arrival of Columbus.

Conrad, Pam. *Pedro's Journal.* New York: Scholastic, Inc.,1992.—Written as a diary by a cabin boy on Columbus's ship.

Schlein, Miram. *I Sailed with Columbus.* New York: Harper Collins, 1991.—Letters written by Julio, a young cabin boy, who sails with Columbus on the *Santa Maria.*

Truce, Henry. *Viking's Dawn.* Washington, D.C.: Phillips, 1956.—The story of early Viking settlements.

HISTORIC SITES TO VISIT

Angel Mounds State Historic Site
8215 Pollack Avenue, Evansville, Indiana 47715
Telephone: (812) 853-3956
Mound builders, called the Mississippians, lived in a village here by the Ohio River.

L'Anse Aux Meadows National Historic Park
P.O. Box 70, St. Lunaire-Griquet
Newfoundland, Canada AOK 2XO
Telephone: (709) 623-2608 or 623-2601
This is believed to be the site of the Viking colony of Vinland.

Sitka National Historical Park
Box 738, Sitka, Alaska 99835
Telephone: (907) 747-6281
The park is known for its collection of totem poles and Northwest Native American crafts.

Castillo de San Marcos
1 Castillo Drive, Saint Augustine, Florida 32084
Telephone: (904) 829-6506
Built by the Spanish, this is the oldest standing fort in the oldest city in the United States.

Roanoke Island Historical Association
Fort Raleigh National Historic Site
1409 Highway 64/264, Manteo,
North Carolina 27954
Telephone: (919) 473-2127
This is the site of the "Lost Colony" of Roanoke Island.

Chaco Culture National Historical Park
P.O. Box 220, Nageezi, New Mexico 87037
Telephone: (505) 786-7014
Pueblo Bonito, a dwelling of the Anasazi, is located here.

INDEX

INDEX